SIR TONY ROBINSON'S
WEIRD WORLD OF WONDERS
PETS

WRITTEN WITH
JESSICA COBB

Illustrated by Del Thorpe

Dedication from the pets of Britain

Thank you for looking after us!

First published 2014 by Macmillan Children's Books

This edition published 2018 by Macmillan Children's Books
a division of Macmillan Publishers Limited
20 New Wharf Road, London N1 9RR
Basingstoke and Oxford
Associated companies throughout the world

www.panmacmillan.com

ISBN 978-1-5098-8978-5

135798642

A CIP catalogue record for this book is available from the British Library.

Typeset by Dan Newman/Perfect Bound Ltd
Printed and bound by CPI Group (UK) Ltd, Croydon CRO 4YY

SIR TONY ROBINSON'S

WEIRD WORLD OF WONDERS

PETS

Other books by Sir Tony Robinson

The Worst Children's Jobs in History

Sir Tony Robinson's Weird World of Wonders: Romans

Sir Tony Robinson's Weird World of Wonders: World War I

Sir Tony Robinson's Weird World of Wonders: World War II

Sir Tony Robinson's Weird World of Wonders: Joke Book

Hello, we're the Curiosity Crew. You'll probably spot us hanging about in this book checking stuff out.

It's about the dog with the longest tongue ever, goldfish who play football, and people who keep hippos as pets.

It's also about a cat who made an entire species extinct, a tortoise who lived to be 250 years old and plenty more besides.

Read on to find out . . .

CHAPTER ONE
WE LOVE PETS!

We love pets!!

But where did they come from?
How smart are they, and what
on earth are they for?

4

CUDDLY WOLVES

Let's start at the beginning with man's oldest and best friend – the dog.

So you should – we're great!

There were over 400 million dogs at the last count.

The reason experts think they're among the very earliest pets is because their remains have been found buried alongside human beings in graves which are thousands of years old.

But dogs haven't always existed. Their story begins 30,000 years ago, deep in the Stone Age, when grey wolves were looking for something juicy to eat, and started sniffing around the places where early humans lived.

IMAGINE YOU'RE A HUNGRY WOLF, AND YOU SNEAK INTO A HUMAN CAMP LOOKING FOR A SMALL CHILD TO NIBBLE.

BUT THEN YOU FEEL THE HEAT FROM THE FIRE, AND SMELL SOMETHING COOKING, MAYBE SOME MAMMOTH STEW OR A TIGER KEBAB, SO YOU DECIDE TO STOP EATING CHILDREN, AND INSTEAD YOU SIT DOWN, OPEN YOUR EYES WIDE, LOOK REALLY CUTE AND FRIENDLY, AND HOPE YOU'LL BE THROWN A BONE OR TWO.

Nice idea. But why didn't the humans chase the wolves away?

Simple – a friendly wolf can be very useful.

It'll eat up all the rotting scraps of food that are lying around.

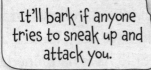
It'll bark if anyone tries to sneak up and attack you.

It'll help you hunt other animals for food.

And if the evening's chilly it'll let you snuggle up to it to keep warm.

Did you know, in some places, when the night gets really cold, local people call it a 'three dog night' because you need at least three dogs cuddling up to you to keep you warm?

Obviously you didn't just snuggle up to any old wolf, not unless you wanted to wake up with no nose. Only the best behaved wolves would have been allowed to hang around the campfire. The ones that ate people would have found themselves turned into wolfskin rugs pretty sharpish.

But the friendly wolves would eventually have had puppies, and the friendliest and most trainable of those puppies would have been looked after by the humans, and this would have happened time after time until the gentler wolves had completely replaced the old kind around the camp and had become a new kind of creature.

A creature we call the dog. This process is known as . . .

EVOLUTION

WHY BEARS TURNED WHITE

Most animals change over time to help them survive in a particular environment.

For example, millions of years ago in the frozen Arctic, bears born with white fur lived for longer, and survived better, than those with brown fur, because their whiteness helped them sneak up on nice, juicy, mouthwatering seals without being noticed. These successful white bears gave birth to other white bears, the brown bears either died out or moved away and eventually all the bears in the Arctic became white 'polar bears'!

Evolution is cool!

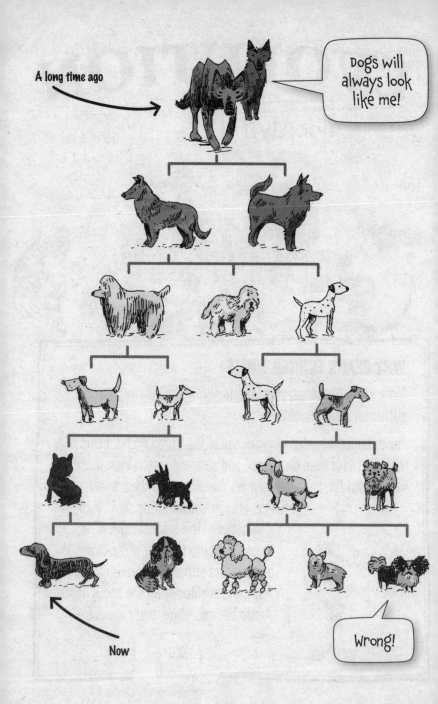

But these changes don't always happen by accident. Humans all over the world have learned how this process works and have deliberately used it to breed all sorts of animals, including lots of different kinds of dogs – big dogs for keeping guard, strong dogs for pulling things, nimble dogs for chasing rats, tiny dogs for looking cute – so today there are hundreds of different types or 'breeds' of dog: from the tiniest Yorkshire Terrier [6.3cm tall] to the largest Great Dane [106.7cm]! . . . but all of them (even the sweetest, fluffiest, smallest, cutest-wootest chihuahua) are descended from grey wolves!

THE SNAKE KILLER

Another creature also started hanging around prehistoric homes, but it wasn't begging for scraps like the wolves were – it was hunting small animals which crawled around the humans' rubbish heaps and grain stores.

African Wild Cats were bigger than modern cats. But like the friendly wolves, they made themselves useful and so weren't chased away. They killed rats and snakes, and prevented mice from stealing the humans' food.

I think he's talking about us.

He's definitely talking about us!

Horrible scary great puss!

Aah, nice little puss!

What's the difference? They're all killers!

12

SHAVING OFF YOUR EYEBROWS

Have you ever lost a cat? If so, I bet you were pretty upset about it. Were you so sad that you shaved off your eyebrows? Probably not. But that's what the ancient Egyptians used to do. They were nutty about cats, who they thought protected them from harm. So they were very sad if their pet cat died, and if it did, out came the razor and shaving soap, and a pair of lovely eyebrows went fluttering to the floor.

13

HOW TO WIN A BATTLE USING CATS

In 525 BC, Persia attacked the Egyptian city of Pelusium. The Persian king knew how soppy the Egyptians were about cats, so he devised a plan: he ordered his soldiers to collect up loads of them, and just before the Persians charged, he released the moggies in front of his attacking army. Rather than run the risk of hurting the cats, the Egyptians immediately surrendered!

By the left, quick —miaow!

But people haven't always loved cats.

Shameless plug – this is from Tony's book about Egyptians. It's great!

BAD NEWS FOR CATS!

In medieval Europe, some people thought that little old ladies were witches and their cats were the devil in disguise.

We're not, honestly!

That's ridiculous!

EVEN WORSE NEWS FOR CATS

When people are scared, they're often really cruel to the thing they're afraid of. And boy, oh boy, were people cruel to medieval cats!

THE CATS GET THEIR OWN BACK

But between the fourteenth and seventeenth centuries, waves of plague swept Europe, human beings got really sick, their bodies erupted in agonizing blisters, and millions of people died.

It wasn't our fault!

No it wasn't, Tiddles. How was the disease spread, Stig?

By fleas that lived on rats.

And why were there so many rats?

Because the stupid humans had killed the cats that should have been chasing them away!

Some people are still weird about cats — especially black ones.

15

Different people in different countries have lots of strange ideas about black cats. Even today animal charities have problems re-homing them because they're believed to be unlucky!

I'm lovely, honestly!

If a black cat crosses your path – that's lucky!

No, if a black cat crosses your path – that's unlucky!

If a black cat walks away from you – that's lucky!

I thought it was unlucky!

It's lucky if one sneezes in your face!

No, that's disgusting!

It's unlucky if you find one in your bed!

And you shouldn't let a black cat in your room while you're having a serious discussion, because it might listen and tell everyone!

That's not lucky or unlucky – it's plain bonkers!!

TONY'S TIPS FOR KEEPING CATS HAPPY!

- When you're introducing your cat to his new home, keep him (or her) indoors for the first two or three weeks, in one room to start with. Give him a nice cosy bed, a scratching post, a  litter tray and a bowl of fresh water. During this time introduce him to new rooms in the house one at a time, until he feels safe and cosy in his new territory.

- Adult cats don't need milk and many of them can get ill from drinking it. Always make sure they have a clean bowl of water to drink from.

- Clean your cat's litter tray every day, as they won't want to use it if it's smelly and dirty.

- Cats need something to scratch, to strengthen their muscles and sharpen their claws. You don't want them scratching your furniture, so give your cat a scratching post which is tall enough for him to use fully stretched.

- If your cat wears a collar, make sure it fits nice and snugly, or get him a quick-release one. If it's too loose a cat can easily get his teeth or claws caught in it when he's cleaning himself, or get caught on a tree branch when he's climbing.

BAKED FLAMINGO

Humans have probably always captured wild birds and turned them into pets. The ancient Romans kept parrots, doves, pigeons, mynah birds, finches, starlings and ravens.

They employed slaves to train us to talk.

They made a big fuss of us.

Unfortunately they liked the way we tasted too – one Roman cookbook gives a recipe for baked parrot . . .

. . . and it says if you run out of parrots you can use a flamingo instead!

They sent us to their friends as birthday presents.

They kept us in cages made of gold or silver.

PIRATES AND PARROTS

After the Roman Empire collapsed, European people didn't have much opportunity to go off hunting for gorgeous animals like parrots. But a thousand years later, faster and stronger ships were invented in which European people could sail to the other side of the world. Some of them wanted to discover new lands, others wanted to find treasure. But the very meanest were pirates who stole whatever treasure they could lay their hands on.

Who's a pretty boy then?

Certainly not you!

Did pirates really keep parrots?

Pirates didn't just make money from raiding other ships. They caught gorgeous, colourful birds, and stuffed cage-loads of them in the holds of their boats so they could sell them back home in Europe.

But a few pirates did actually keep them as pets. They taught the birds swear words and rude songs to help pass the time on their long voyages.

Go on then, sing something.

That's disgusting!

*********!!!

Parrots weren't the only popular foreign birds. In 1402 the Spanish took over the Canary Islands off the coast of Africa, and discovered that the birds who lived there could sing really well. So they caught some and took them back with them to Spain. They named them 'canaries' after the islands, and the birds became a big hit in Europe.

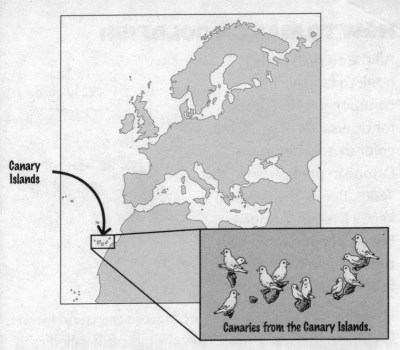

Canary Islands

Canaries from the Canary Islands.

In the eighteenth century people even sold little organs called 'serinettes', which they wound up and played, to encourage their birdies to sing along to the latest tunes.

Dost thou know anything by One Direction?

HOW TO MAKE A GOLDFISH

All the animals in this book so far have been common pets in Europe for thousands of years, but goldfish only became a European pet fashion in the 1600s. Before then if you'd kept a live fish in your house, people would have thought you were either a fishmonger or bonkers!

We look really cool!

It was the ancient Chinese who started the trend for keeping underwater pets. They thought fish called carp were very tasty, and reared them for food. But they discovered that every now and again the carp had little orange or gold babies. They liked them so much that they started breeding the prettiest fish, and kept them in china bowls so they could watch them swim about (they hadn't invented telly yet).

When Europeans first saw pictures of these beautiful fish, they thought they were mythical creatures that an artist had made up. Then when they were shipped to Europe and it became obvious they were real, people called them goldfish and they became all the rage.

There was a big problem though. Goldfish don't survive long in a glass bowl. The water becomes stagnant unless you change it regularly and the fish die. It wasn't until 1850 that scientist Robert Warington worked out that putting plants in the water helped give the fish more oxygen and kept them alive for longer.

And that was the beginning of aquariums.

HOLD YOUR HORSES!

Have we missed a pet out?

For 5,000 years horses have been ever present in human history: domesticating them was one of the most important things to human civilization. They have been our companions in times of war and peace. They pulled chariots, carts, carriages and wagons. They delivered post and provisions and people. They were used for farming, sport and hunting. In a time before trains, cars and planes they were vital for travel and communication.

Now they are used mainly for sport – jumping, eventing, racing, dressage and recreation.

But are they pets? Only for a few lucky people . . .

BUCEPHALUS THE GREAT

The brilliant Greek general Alexander the Great had a horse called Bucephalus. The general was the only person who could keep him calm. He worked out that the horse was afraid of his own shadow, so he always turned Bucephalus towards the sun . . . that way his shadow stayed behind him.

Alexander loved his horse so much that when Bucephalus was stolen, he threatened to destroy the whole country unless the horse was returned, which he promptly was!

When Bucephalus finally died, Alexander built a city named after him – Bucephala.

DO YOU LIKE BUNNIES?

DO YOU THINK THEY'RE SWEET?

DO YOU THINK THEY'RE REALLY, REALLY SWEET?

THEN MAYBE YOU SHOULD MISS OUT THE NEXT TWO PARAGRAPHS.

In days gone by, why did people keep rabbits? Because they were fluffy and had little pink noses? No – they put them in a pot, cooked them and ate them. The meat from one rabbit could feed a whole family. Plus, rabbits breed lots of baby rabbits very quickly – which meant you could have rabbit stew the whole year long. And their fur could be made into cosy, snug clothes.

It was the Romans who first started keeping them in big numbers. They discovered thousands of wild bunnies hopping around in Spain and decided to make money out of them. They set up rabbit farms surrounded by deep walls to stop them burrowing out and escaping, and soon had more rabbits than you could possibly imagine.

In fact some people say that the name 'Spain' comes from the Latin word 'Hispania' meaning 'Land of the Rabbits'!

THE CRAZE FOR CUTE BUNNIES

In the sixteenth century bunnies became a big craze – rich Italian women kept them as house-pets, spoilt them and even wrote sad poems about them when they died. But the bunny rabbit craze didn't take off in the UK until over 200 years later in Victorian times. Children were given rabbits as pets, and even adults took a fancy to them, breeding different types and entering them in competitions to judge which was the prettiest, or the fattest, or had the biggest ears.

BENJAMIN'S BUTTERED TOAST

Have you heard of the writer Beatrix Potter? When she was growing up she kept lots of pets including frogs, a tortoise, a bat, mice, hedgehogs and rabbits. One of her favourite rabbits was called Benjamin Bouncer, and she'd take him for walks on a little lead. She told people he used to rush into the dining room whenever he heard the tea bell, because he was so fond of the buttered toast on the tea tray. Her pets inspired her to write a series of children's books about animals.

Never mind the buttered toast — I fancy some cabbage!

QUIZ

Finish the titles of these Beatrix Potter books:

THE TALE OF PETER . . .
a) Crocodile **b)** The Potato **c)** Rabbit
d) Piper

THE TALE OF BENJAMIN . . .
a) Big Nose **b)** The Banana **c)** Bunny
d) Bossy Boots

THE TALE OF TWO BAD . . .
a) Eggs **b)** Mice **c)** Tummy Aches
d) Boys Who Stuck Their Tongues Out

THE TALE OF LITTLE PIG . . .
a) Robinson **b)** Tony Robinson **c)** Bobbinson
d) Flobbinson

THE TALE OF JEREMY . . .
a) Clarkson **b)** Jughandle **c)** Fisher
d) Jellybottom

Did you know that guinea pigs were kept for food too? Even today lots of people still eat guinea pig – in Peru they munch about 65 million of them every year!

Eat him, he's fatter than me!

Ooh no – I'm all skin and bone!

Have you looked at your tum lately?

Did you know? Guinea pigs should really be called 'not-guinea-not-pigs', because they aren't pigs, and aren't from Guinea. We don't know where the name came from. Perhaps when they first arrived in Europe people believed they came from the country of Guinea in Africa, and thought they were little pigs because they made squealing noises.

In the sixteenth century, European explorers brought guinea pigs back to Europe, and because they were small, cute, furry and easy to look after, they quickly became popular, not as tasty snacks, but as pets. Even Queen Elizabeth I owned one.

Tony Robinson

Yoo-hoo!

OK, now for a personal admission. I love guinea pigs. I used to own not one . . . not two . . . but TEN of them. They were called Angel, Baby, Jazzy, Mr B, Amber, Sienna, Dopes, Lola, Myrtle and Pearly-poo.

I'm Baby!

I'm Angel!

TONY'S TIPS FOR MAKING YOUR GUINEA PIG HAPPY

- Guinea pigs are sociable animals and don't like being on their own. Keep at least two if you can – in as big a cage as possible.

Make sure they're females or the male is neutered, or you'll soon be up to your neck in tiny piggies!!

- It's good to get your new guinea pigs from a rescue centre rather than a pet shop, as there are so many that need new homes.

- Keep your pigs indoors if you can, especially in winter. That way they won't get cold and you'll get to know them better.

Let me in!

- The best type of hay is called 'Western Timothy'. Ordinary hay can make them wheezy, as it's full of spores and mites.

- Give them a plastic or cardboard box to shelter in – it makes them feel cosy and safe.

- Give them fresh fruit, veg and water every day, and premixed dry food so they get all the goodness they possibly can.

I'm crazy about parsley!

LILAC MICE

Most people throughout history have thought of mice as pests. This is due to their amazing ability to squeeze through small spaces, nibble through hard-to-open containers, and gobble up human food supplies. To try and stop them, people put down poison, set traps and bought cats to chase them. But, every now and again, someone, somewhere, decided they'd make really good pets.

Pet mice were first kept in the ancient Far East. In Japan white mice were believed to be messengers from the God of Good Fortune, so keeping one was a way of giving yourself good luck. Later, different-coloured mice became popular – black ones, silver, chocolate brown, lilac and even albino (white with red eyes). These cute little squeakers were known as 'fancy mice'!

Ooh, look! Fancy mice!

Yes, I really fancy mice!

CHAPTER TWO
PET SKILLZ

Our own pets may not seem quite as talented as elephants, seals and mimic octopuses, but they have some pretty amazing skills.

I can detect water up to twelve miles away.

I can slow my heartbeat from 125 beats per minute to about ten, so I need less oxygen and can stay underwater for longer.

I can change my colour and texture to blend into my surroundings, I can also copy the behaviour of at least fifteen different other animals like jelly fish, stingrays and shrimps.

Nits's only amazing skill is being able to eat an entire Sunday roast off the side when nobody's looking and then do bottom-burps that smell of roast potatoes.

You underestimate me! We dogs can't see as well as you, but we have a brilliant sense of hearing.

We can detect sounds four times further away than you can, and move our ears to pinpoint exactly where the noise is coming from.

A dog's sense of smell is even more incredible – it's thousands of times more sensitive than yours or mine. For example, dogs can smell a teaspoon of sugar in a container of water the size of two swimming pools!

Yum, I can smell curry!

Oh really! I can smell garlic, turmeric, onions, tomatoes, cumin, coriander, chillies, yogurt, pepper, salt . . .

TONY'S TAJ

FIVE TOP THINGS DOGS CAN SMELL

DVDs – Dogs can be taught to smell the material that DVDs are made out of so the police can hunt down fakes. In one police raid in Malaysia, dogs found a pile of pirated DVDs worth over $3 million!

Drowned bodies – Believe it or not, dogs can smell through water, so they're used to recover the bodies of people who have drowned.

Aargh!

Bed Bugs – Pest control services use them to search hotel rooms for bed bugs.

Booby traps – Dogs are used by the army to detect enemy booby traps. They need to be silent in order not to alert the enemy, so they're taught to warn their handlers of danger by crossing their ears or raising the hairs on their necks. One dog was taught to stand up on its hind legs when a booby trap was nearby!

Cancer – Dogs can even smell human illnesses! Some have been trained to sniff people's breath and alert them if they smell cancer.

HOW A DOG SMELLS

Wet nose – This wetness helps a dog capture tiny scent particles.

Nostrils – Dogs can wiggle their nostrils to work out which direction a smell's coming from.

Smell Receptors – At the back of a dog's nose are lots of special scent receptors which pick out all the different smells in the air.

HOW MANY SCENT RECEPTORS HAVE YOU GOT?

I've got 5 million – awesome!

I've got 147 million!

I've got 225 million!

I've got 300 million! Stig, you're rubbish!

Yes, bloodhounds are super-trackers – they've been used for centuries to find escaped prisoners, missing people, lost children and even other pets. They've been known to find a target over 100 miles away just by following its smell!

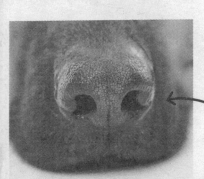

Did you know that a dog's nose print is like a human's fingerprint? Every single one is different!

CAT ATTACK

Cats have a great sense of smell too, not to mention a whole host of other incredible talents . . .

Night vision – Cats' eyes are specially designed to let in more light than ours, so they can see more in the dark.

Ultrasonic hearing – This allows them to hear sounds that we can't, like the very high-pitched squeak of a mouse.

Whiskers – To sense air currents and the location of objects in the dark.

Razor sharp claws – To enable them to climb trees. They can also draw in their claws for silent stalking.

Flexible backbone and lightning reflexes – Which allow a cat to spin round quickly and right itself if it falls through the air. Cats are often said to have 'nine lives' because they're so good at surviving falls from a great height.

Powerful hind legs – They can jump up to five times their own height! (That's like us being able to leap on to the roof of a two-storey house.)

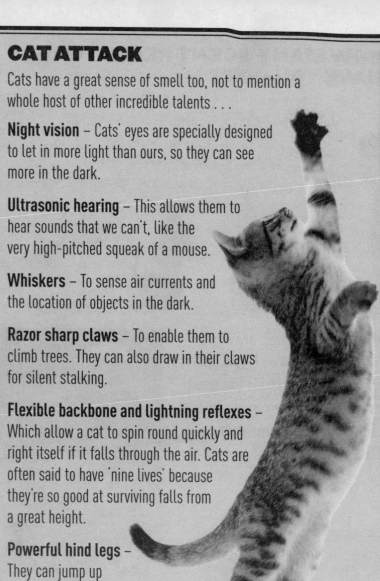

All these skills make your pet cat a highly efficient killer. There's nothing cats do better than hunt and kill small furry creatures. In America scientists reckon pet cats kill over 2 billion birds and 12 billion small animals every year!

Sorry – it was an accident!

They're so efficient that in some parts of the world, they've managed to wipe out whole species of animals!

Not on purpose, honestly!

'Stephens Island wrens' were small flightless songbirds found on an island near New Zealand – that is until the lighthouse keeper's cat Tibbles arrived in 1894 and started catching and eating them. The wren became famous for being the only species to have been made completely extinct by one single animal!

We really should have learned how to fly . . .

Or gone by car.

BORN SURVIVORS

Cats may be hard-wired to kill, but rabbits are designed to stay alive.

All-round vision –
Except for a small spot on the bridge of their nose, rabbits can see all around them. Useful when on the look out for their enemies.

Large powerful hind legs –
They can stand up, look out for attackers and if they spot any, can run really fast to get away from them. They can reach speeds of up to 45mph and can zigzag, bound and leap over obstacles.

Large long ears –
To detect predators.

White fluffy tail – When a rabbit runs away, its tail seems to appear and disappear, confusing any animal chasing it.

RABBIT SHOW-JUMPING

Did you know that rabbits are so good at running and jumping that in some countries people hold Rabbit Show-Jumping competitions with miniature jumps, ramps and hurdles? The highest recorded jump by a rabbit is one metre, and their record for the long jump is three metres.

ANOTHER WHERE THAT CAME FROM

If all else fails and a rabbit gets eaten, the good news is there are lots more rabbits, because the other thing that rabbits are really, really good at is making babies. A mummy rabbit can give birth to up to forty baby rabbits each year.

In 1859 the first twenty-four rabbits were brought to Australia.

That's a lot of nappies!

By 1959 the original twenty-four had become 600 million!

THE DREADED SWAMP RABBIT

Rabbits aren't normally known for their violent tendencies – but every now and again along comes a story of an attack by a killer rabbit . . . dum-dum-duuuum!

In 1979 the President of the United States, Jimmy Carter, went fishing, and a giant swamp rabbit jumped into the water and swam towards his boat hissing menacingly. The President splashed at it with his paddle until it swam away. Next day a newspaper headline read: 'President Attacked by Rabbit!'

Swamp rabbits exist – honestly! They live in America and they're big and have waterproof fur so they can swim and dive under water!

Jimmy Carter isn't the only famous historical figure to have been threatened by rabbits. In 1807, the great military leader and French Emperor Napoleon Bonaparte held a rabbit hunt. Unfortunately the organizers used tame rabbits instead of wild ones and, when they were released, they ran back in the direction of the hunters looking for something to eat. Hundreds of them stormed towards Napoleon who was forced to race back to his carriage to escape the horde of hungry hoppers.

Tee-hee-hee!

TONY'S TIPS
FOR MAKING YOUR
RABBIT HAPPY

- In the wild, rabbits live in large groups and hop around a territory the size of thirty football pitches. Letting one live on its own in a tiny hutch is just mean.

A nice big cage please!

- You'd get bored sitting around all day in your room – and so do rabbits. Give them big cages.

- Make them tunnels, platforms for hiding under and climbing on, and a box filled with earth for digging. Change things around every now and again to give them a bit of variety. For instance, put food in several places so they have to hop around looking for it.

Something to play with please!

- Try training your rabbit. Use treats to encourage it to poo in a litter tray. Encourage it to stand up on its rear legs for a piece of food. But remember, never shout or punish it or it'll get scared!

- You'll know if your rabbit is really happy. It'll do a special jump and twist which is known as a 'binky'.

Hooray!!

SMART PETS

OK, so I know you're smart – you must be because you're reading this book. But do you know just how smart pets are?

Dogs can understand over 165 words and gestures, and some can recognize as many as 250. They can also count up to five.

Your average dog is as intelligent as a two-year-old child.

One – two – three – four – Er . . . !

One – two – three – four – Er . . . !

OK, maybe that's not A-level standard, but it's pretty impressive for an animal that sniffs lamp posts.

I can do that too!

Cats are very smart, but just how smart is difficult to measure. For example, in one test cats and dogs were put in mazes to see how long it would take them to find their way out in return for a treat. The dogs sniffed around and eventually got their reward . . .

Cos we're really brainy!

... but the cats just sat and washed themselves.

No – we were just too smart to take part in such a stupid test! We knew if we stood still long enough the humans would give us a treat anyway!

And what about fish?

Durr!!

Scientists used to think the memory of a goldfish only lasted for about three seconds ... but they were wrong. We now know that there are some things they can remember for at least three months.

Hey, I've just remembered I'm brainy!

They recognize faces and can even be taught to tell the time.

Scientists have taught some fish to collect their own food by pressing a small lever in their tank at a particular time of day.

An American goldfish called Comet has been trained to be an athlete. He can play football and basketball, he can swim round a series of poles, and push a miniature rugby ball over a set of posts!

AMAZING GOLDFISH SURVIVAL STORIES

Goldfish are really tough! Some of us have survived out of water for several hours!

. . . like me, Ginger. I spent thirteen hours behind a cupboard before my owner found me and popped me back in my bowl.

I'm Bercy. When I was 4 years old I was in a car crash and was thrown through the window on to a busy motorway. Police found me still alive 15ft away on the tarmac!

We can survive in these conditions because if our gills are wet we can still take in oxygen.

But it's pretty stressful – please don't try it with your pet fish!

TONY'S TIPS FOR LOOKING AFTER YOUR GOLDFISH

- Don't put sand in the bottom of your tank or bowl . . .

  . . . use 2–3mm sized gravel instead.

- Never remove all the gravel when you're cleaning out your tank. There are healthy bacteria in it that keep the water clean.

  It cuts our mouths!

- Use an air pump or special filter instead of plants to put oxygen into the water.

  Because we eat the plants or dig them out!

- Add rocks or ornaments specially made for fish tanks. They give the fish somewhere to shelter.

  And they look pretty!

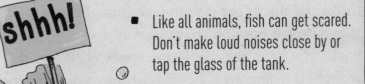

shhh!

- Like all animals, fish can get scared. Don't make loud noises close by or tap the glass of the tank.

WHO'S A CLEVER BIRDIE?

Parrots are head and shoulders above all other pets when it comes to intelligence tests. An African Grey called Alex (short for '**A**vian **L**anguage **Ex**periment') who lived in a lab in America, could say over 100 words, recognize fifty different objects and seven colours, and count up to eight.

He even helped teach other parrots. He would ask them questions, squawk '*Say better*' when they got words wrong, and even gave them clues about the correct answer – like hissing '*ssss*' when the answer was 'seven'.

Who's a naughty boy? Alex!

If he asked for a banana and got a nut instead, he'd throw the nut at the person who brought it to him. When he got bored with his tests and wanted to be put back in his cage he'd say '*Wanna go back*'. If that didn't work he'd deliberately give the wrong answers to the questions. He wasn't always difficult though. When he knew he'd been badly behaved, he'd say '*I'm sorry*'.

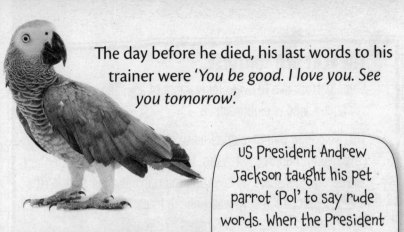

The day before he died, his last words to his trainer were '*You be good. I love you. See you tomorrow*'.

US President Andrew Jackson taught his pet parrot 'Pol' to say rude words. When the President died, Pol attended his funeral, but had to be sent out the room . . . because he was swearing so loudly!

You slay me.

President Andrew Jackson, 1840.

I'm XXXXing hysterical!

THE VERY OLD TORTOISE

Some parrots live to over eighty years of age. The world's oldest is Poncho, who is eighty-seven.

That's nothing though compared to other long-lived pets. Koi carp live for hundreds of years. How do we know? Because their age can be measured by counting the rings on their scales. The oldest recorded Koi carp was Hanako (meaning 'Flower Maid') from Japan. She died in 1977 aged 226 years!

But even older than Hanako was Adwaita, a 250kg tortoise. In the eighteenth century he belonged to the British general Robert Clive. Adwaita didn't die until 2006, so he must have lived for over 250 years!

THE NOISIEST CAT

OK, so your own pet may not be mega-intelligent – it probably can't talk, play basketball or find its way out of a maze in a month of Sundays. But maybe it's got a secret skill you haven't discovered yet. You never know, perhaps it could even be a record breaker like one of these . . .

Longest dog tongue: Puggy the Pekinese from Texas has a tongue which is 4.5 inches long.

Most tennis balls in mouth: Augie, a golden retriever, can hold five tennis balls in her mouth at the same time.

Longest cat: Stewie measures 48.5 inches long – or just over 4 feet (which is the height of an average eight-year-old child!)

Most flying discs caught: Rose the Labrador can hold on to seven frisbees without dropping them.

Most balloons popped: Anastasia the Jack Russell terrier can pop a hundred balloons in 44.49 seconds.

Loudest purr: Smokey the grey tabby cat can purr up to 92.7 decibels, which is as loud as a lawnmower or a hairdryer.

Even if your pet is no good at breaking records, you can still give it a record-breaking name. The nineteenth-century poet Robert Southey named one of his cats 'His Serene Highness, the Archduke Rumpelstiltskin, Marquis Macbum, Earl Tomlemange, Baron Raticide, Waouler ad Skaratsch' . . . Try engraving that on a cat collar.

CHAPTER THREE

WHO INVENTED THE KING CHARLES SPANIEL?

Suppose you woke up one morning, and a royal messenger burst into your bedroom and announced that you'd just been made King or Queen!

About time too!

Suppose they whisked you away in a golden carriage to Westminster Abbey, sat you on a throne, stuck a crown on your head and gave you the keys to Buckingham Palace!

Ta very much.

You'd be well chuffed, wouldn't you? Suddenly you'd be super rich, no one would moan at you if you left your shoes lying about, servants would rush out and get you a takeaway whenever you wanted ... What's not to like?

Sounds great!

There is that . . .

Nothing! – Except that after a few days you'd get a bit lonely and very, very bored. You'd be spending all your time opening flower shows, shaking people's hands, and being talked at by posh people with la-di-da accents.

You'd probably want a friend, a pet maybe, that you could cuddle, and make a fuss of.

DOGS IN A BASKET

Louis XV of France became king when he was very young. His mum, dad and brother were dead, so he

got extremely lonely. But never mind – at least he had his pet dog.

My doggie's the only thing in the world that likes me for myself!

Actually I'm not that keen on him.

He treated his little four-legged friend like a prince, gave him a velvet cushion for a bed, and a gold collar studded with diamonds. He was just as soppy about his cats.

Louis XV getting crowned, aged eleven.

59

King Henry III (also of France) owned a staggering 300 tiny dogs! Each time he and his wife Queen Louise went out for their daily walk, they'd take a few of them out in a specially made basket that hung round Henry's neck!

300 dogs, honest – count them!

Sorry, it was only 295.

Whoops, sorry we were late!

But it wasn't just French royalty who were daft about their pets.

Mary, Queen of Scots owned over twenty little white Maltese lap dogs. When she was beheaded in 1587, one dog crawled out from between the folds of her clothes, lay next to her severed head and refused to budge.

Queen Alexandra (on the right), wife of King Edward VII, with one of her dogs. She allowed them to walk on the dining table, and eat off the plates.

My dogs give me so much pleasure.

You wouldn't know it.

In the seventeenth century, the English King Charles II kept lots of little dogs which went with him everywhere. Not everybody liked them. One visitor complained that the King was always messing around with his dogs instead of paying attention to important royal business!

There was one particular breed of spaniel that King Charles really liked. Guess what it was called.

Were they called floppy-eared spaniels?

Or brown and white spaniels?

How about big-eyed glum spaniels?

The clue's in his name, dummies!

Your Majesty, there appears to be a three-headed dog under your feet!

Never mind that. Do you like my moustache?

Royal pets can often get away with being really badly behaved. In Germany, Kaiser Wilhelm II's dachshunds snapped at people's ankles, nipped at their clothes, clawed the furniture and piddled everywhere. If anyone complained, the Kaiser just laughed!

63

The English King Edward VII's white fox terrier, called Caesar, chewed men's trouser legs and was always running off to hunt rabbits and birds. He once disappeared during a royal visit and a whole police force was sent to find him! It wasn't hard; he wore a collar which said ...

'I AM CAESAR I BELONG TO THE KING'

I don't want to stand up. Caesar's eaten the bottoms of my trouser-legs!

And very tasty they were too!

WILLS'S CIGARETTES.

FUNERAL OF EDWARD VII.

Where's the coffin gone? Where's it gone!

When Edward VII died, Caesar was heartbroken and spent days outside his master's bedroom door, whining and refusing to eat. At the King's funeral he was given the honour of walking behind the coffin.

But it wasn't just dogs that were popular in royal circles.

Charles XII of Sweden had a favourite cat which used to lie on his desk and sleep on his papers. Rather than disturb him, the King wrote around the cat, leaving a blank cat-shape on his letters!

Queen Elizabeth of Bohemia was famous for keeping pet monkeys. People said she liked them better than her own children.

Maybe I did!

TONY'S TIPS TO KEEP YOUR DOG HAPPY

- A dog needs a comfortable, dry, draught-free, clean and quiet place to snooze in. Dogs like to turn around before settling so make sure you choose a dog bed that's big enough.

- Always make sure it's got clean water to drink. Change its water regularly, because dogs often drop bits of food into it when they are eating . . .

. . . and that makes the water go bad!

- Brush your dog gently and often; it's very good for its coat, and can get rid of loose hairs and dirt which otherwise would end up all over your home.

Remember we can be ticklish too!

- Some dogs suffer with bad teeth. You can give them a special daily chew which will help to clean them. Maybe try brushing your puppy's teeth with special meat-flavoured toothpaste. Ask your vet to show you how.

- Dogs need to go to the toilet several times a day. So make sure you take them for plenty of walks or allow them out into the garden as often as they need.

And remember: always pick up our poo in a bag and put it in a bin.

PANTHERS IN THE PALACE

Other monarchs had much more exotic pets than dogs!

King Haile Selassie of Ethiopia kept lions, tigers and panthers, which he allowed to roam through his palace.

European kings and queens often had their own zoos – or 'menageries' (pronounced 'men-aj-erries'), where they used to keep the wild or unusual animals given to them by their royal mates in other countries.

In London, there was a royal menagerie at the Tower of London. It housed lions, tigers, elephants, kangaroos and ostriches. Back in the thirteenth century it even housed a polar bear which had been given to the King of England by the King of Norway. It was kept on a long lead and allowed to fish in the River Thames!

The Tower menagerie was closed in 1835, and the remaining animals were moved to London Zoo.

King Haile Selassie with one of his pet lions.

The Tower of London.

GGRRRR!

HISSS!

SQUEAK!

WHOOP-WHOOP!

ROARR!

WHINNY!

CHIRP!

A CANDLE IN YOUR MOUTH

Halt! Who miaows there?

Not all royal pets sat around looking cute and interesting. Some of them had jobs to do.

- In eighteenth-century France, poodles at the palace of Versailles carried the edges of their mistresses' long skirts in their mouths to prevent them tripping.

- Unpopular kings or queens like Carlota, Empress of Mexico, used dogs and cats to taste their food to check it hadn't been poisoned!

- In Thailand, Siamese cats were used to guard royal palaces and temples. These fierce pussies sat on high walls and mewed loudly when intruders came near.

69

- Before burglar alarms were invented, dogs were often used as royal security guards. In England in 1549, King Edward VI's life was saved when his pet dog heard an intruder and started barking. His barks alerted the guards and the would-be assassin was arrested . . . but unfortunately in the commotion the dog was killed!

ONCE UPON A TIME IN THE THIRTEENTH CENTURY . . .

. . . Prince Llewelyn of North Wales went hunting, but left his faithful hound, Gelert, behind.

When he returned home, he found his son's cradle overturned and Gelert covered in blood. He plunged his sword into the dog believing that it had killed his little boy. The dog's dying scream was answered by a baby's cry. Behind the cradle Llewelyn found his son unharmed and nearby was the body of a mighty wolf that Gelert had slain to protect the child. Llewelyn was so upset he never smiled again.

A DOG CALLED DASH

Queen Victoria was a big animal lover – one of her earliest pets was a spaniel called Dash. The two were inseparable and on special occasions she used to dress him in a little jacket and trousers.

When she was eighteen, she was made queen, and on the day she was crowned, she rushed back after the ceremony to give Dash his bath.

Queen Victoria and her husband Albert playing with their pets.

By the end of her reign Victoria had eighty-eight pet dogs! She ordered pictures to be painted of her favourites and entered the best-looking ones in dog shows. She even had a little cottage built next to the royal kennels so she could sit in it and watch her doggie chums scampering around.

When Dash died in 1840, Victoria had him buried in Windsor Park with a marble sculpture on top of his grave. Several of her other dogs were later buried alongside him, including Sharp, her border collie.

POINTED EARS

But Queen Victoria's dogs weren't the first or last pets to be given a grand burial.

- Pointed Ears was a royal guard dog who lived over 4,000 years ago in ancient Egypt. When he died, he was wrapped in fine linen, a big ceremony was held in his honour, and he was put in a royal coffin inside a stone tomb built for him near the pyramids. Only the most important humans got this kind of treatment. He must have been a seriously good guard dog.

We may not look it, but we are rather amused.
I'm glad someone is.
I've never hidden under a queen's skirt before.
Great, isn't it?

- King Frederick the Great took burying his pets one step further. He loved his eleven hunting dogs so much that he had them buried at his summer palace. Each one was under its own marble slab, and before he died, he asked to be buried alongside them!

At first this request wasn't granted: he was buried in a church at Potsdam. But 200 years later he was reburied at his summer palace next to his dogs; so his wish finally came true!

- In England in 1914, when Queen Alexandra's favourite little dog Togo died, she had him put on a pillow in her bedroom. He lay there for two days and was only buried after he started to smell like an egg sandwich.

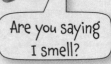

Are you saying I smell?

AND NOW, THE NUTTIEST RULERS OF ALL . . .

If you think those monarchs were a bit bonkers about their pets – you ain't heard nothing yet!

- The Roman Emperor Caligula used to feed his favourite horse, Swift, on flakes of pure gold.

Glittery poo – great!

74

I'm dead scary, me.

- In ancient China, Pekinese dogs belonging to the Emperor had their own bodyguards to accompany them on walks, and their own personal servants to wait on them hand and foot. The penalty for stealing one of these pampered pooches from the royal palace was death by ten thousand slices!

- The Maharaja (or King) of Junagadh in India owned 800 dogs. Each one had its own room, servant and telephone! In 1922 the Maharaja 'married' his favourite dog Roshanara to a golden retriever called Bobby. The three-day ceremony cost £22,000, and was attended by thousands of guests, including 250 dogs dressed in jewels and riding on elephants!

How was your day, darling?

CHAPTER FOUR

NITS'S GUIDE TO 'PET-CESSORIES'

Look at this stuff! For thousands of years, we dogs have been given fancy accessories to wear. Expensive collars have always been in fashion.

This brass collar is French and over 300 years old.

For example, archaeologists found a beautiful leather dog collar from ancient Egypt. It was over 3,000 years old and decorated with a hunting scene.

But not all early collars were made of leather. The remains of a dog from ancient China were discovered wearing one made of gold, silver and precious stones! It was buried alongside a king who lived over 2,300 years ago.

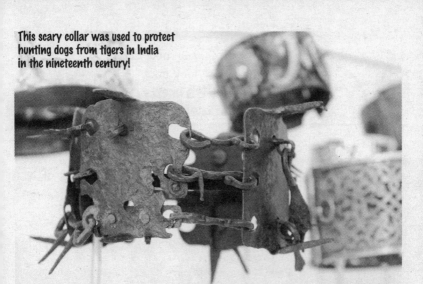

This scary collar was used to protect hunting dogs from tigers in India in the nineteenth century!

Hunting dogs used to wear spiked collars to protect them from attacks by wolves and bears. But this kind of collar carried on being popular throughout history (even when wolves and bears became scarce) because they made us look extra fierce.

Some pet owners took this look a step further and dressed us in actual armour! The set of doggy armour over the page was made for a pampered pet in the seventeenth century.

Doggy armour may look cool but it's pretty useless.

It makes it hard for us to see or move, and that rather ruins the point of it!

While some humans wanted their dogs to look scary, others liked to deck them out in ribbons and bows so they'd look pretty. This painting of dogs belonging to a wealthy seventeenth century Italian family shows them dressed in daft little ruffs! Pretty humiliating – eh, guys?

What every seventeenth-century woman needs: a dog with a pierced ear! (P. Mignard – Henriette d'Orleans)

More doggy bling from the Dog Collar Museum in Leeds (yes that's right, there truly is an actual museum of dog collars).

Today if your master or mistress is stinking rich and a bit daft they can spend millions on a collar for you. The most expensive one currently on sale is encrusted with 1,600 diamonds and would cost you about £2 million!

But dogs haven't just been given bling to make them look good. We've been dressed up and fluffed up, primped and preened, brushed and sprayed, and clipped and curled!

For instance, 150 years ago in London and Paris you'd find 'Dogs' Toilet Clubs'. These were doggy grooming salons where you got taken for an egg-yolk shampoo, a scented bath or a manicure. And if your owner wanted something even more posh, they'd sort you out with pretty patterns shaved into your coat!

But the Victorians weren't the first to pimp their pooches. The ancient Romans were doing daft things to us over 2,000 years ago. They groomed their poodles to look like lions, with a shaved body and big fuzzy mane around their head.

...and this is what they did to poodles in the middle of the twentieth century!

I said a LITTLE off the back!

Not content with bling and paint spray, some owners dress their pets in a variety of ridiculous outfits.

Coats for dogs have been around for a long while. Medieval kings sometimes dressed their favourite dogs in natty jackets to keep them warm in their draughty castles.

82

But even medieval kings weren't daft enough to start putting hats and shoes on their animals. Nope, that was left to the Victorians. They went completely bananas with clothes for their pets.

If you were rich you could buy a whole wardrobe of clobber for your pampered pooch – a fur coat, boots, a pocket handkerchief, lace underwear and even a doggy umbrella (to stop your doggy's designer fur coat getting wet).

One animal fashion expert said that dogs should have a different outfit for day and evening, a cloak for travelling (complete with a pocket to keep their train ticket in), and a little sailor's outfit for the beach!

In the 1930s, novelist Elinor Glyn was famous for going out to lunch with her cat Candide draped around her neck like a scarf!

And it didn't just stop there. People went on dressing up their dogs right through into the twentieth century. Some people even used their pets as fashion accessories.

Today pet fashion is a multi-million-pound industry. Cities like New York and Moscow even hold pet fashion weeks where we have to parade in a range of crazy costumes and designer outfits. But is all this dressing up good for us?

CHAPTER FIVE
Bizarre
PETS

 Some people dress their pets in wacky outfits in order to attract attention . . .

 But others go even further . . .

 They get themselves a wacky pet!

 Everyone knows somebody with a little playmate like me!

Throughout history people have owned rare pets, but they can be dangerous. Many of these cute critters would be more than happy to bite their owner, trash his house . . . and even worse!

TOP FIVE BIZARRE PETS

No. 5: MONKEYS

NOVELTY VALUE: 2 out of 10
Monkeys may seem unusual pets, but people have been keeping them for thousands of years.

POO-FLINGING VALUE: 10 out of 10
They like dangling from light fittings, and flinging their poo on the floor.

TOTAL: 12

Louis XV of Spain, aged four, in 1714.

Before zoos and the Discovery Channel were invented, not many people got to see exotic animals. So if you walked around with a pet monkey on a lead, it would get you noticed. In medieval times, kings and queens often owned monkeys in order to show their subjects how rich and extravagant they were. They even posed with their pets for expensive oil paintings.

This is Catherine of Aragon, who was married to the English King Henry VIII.

As you can probably see from her face, she wasn't a happy queen.

She got very homesick and kept a monkey to remind her of her Spanish homeland where monkeys lived wild and free.

Monkeys look a bit like little versions of us, so their antics make humans laugh. They're smart, they can be taught to do tricks and imitate people. The ancient Romans used to dress them up in hats and tunics, taught them to play musical instruments and trained them to ride goats and throw spears. But as many a monkey-owner has found out, monkeys often turn out to be more trouble than they're worth. A twelfth-century writer said . . .

The monkey is a tricky animal with bad habits. However much it might be tamed, it is always wild. It is playful with the small offspring of humans and dogs, but it sometimes strangles unguarded boys, and hurls them from a great height.

The monkeys he was writing about weren't being naughty; they were just unhappy and cross because they weren't allowed to be free. But people didn't realize this and punished them for their anti-social behaviour.

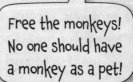

I definitely don't want one now!

Free the monkeys! No one should have a monkey as a pet!

But however much of a nuisance pet monkeys might be, it hasn't stopped more recent celebrities jumping on the monkey-owning bandwagon.

Unfortunately lots of people think owning a pet monkey is cool. So every year thousands of baby monkeys get taken away from their mothers and their nice warm jungles, and are shipped to Europe and America where people lock them in cages, keep them as pets, and stuff them full of bananas.

BUBBLES

One massively successful chimp-owning celebrity was Michael Jackson. His pet was called Bubbles, and he slept in a cot next to the singer's bed. The two friends went everywhere together, until eventually baby Bubbles grew into a not-so-cute 160lb aggressive adult male. In 1988 there was a rumour that he attacked his master, and eventually had to be moved to an animal sanctuary where he's spent the rest of his life happily munching on sweet potatoes and watching TV.

Bananas might sound fine, but in the wild, we don't just eat fruit, we eat lots of different things like plants, insects and small animals.

Making us only eat bananas is like making you only eat Brussels sprouts.

Some pet monkeys even have their teeth removed or filed down to stop them biting people.

No. 4: SQUIRRELS

NOVELTY VALUE: 6 out of 10

Squirrels may be pretty common in parks and gardens, but how many times have you seen one on a lead?

GNAWING & SKIN-SHREDDING VALUE: 10 out of 10

There are lots of old paintings of these cute little bundles of fur and teeth with their owners. Often the squirrel is attached to a tiny chain to stop it scampering off.

TOTAL: 16

> Ok, so they're not as exotic as monkeys, but if you took one for a stroll round your local shopping centre, I bet you'd raise a few eyebrows.

> Stop tickling – I'm trying to keep a straight face.

> There must be some nuts in here somewhere!

A sixteenth-century lady with a squirrel and a starling.

In the 1700s, Americans often raided squirrel nests to steal the babies and sell them at the local market as pets. Some became so tame that they would sit on young boys' shoulders and follow them everywhere.

This is cool!

No, it's cruel!

A boy called Henry Pelham with a squirrel, 1765.

But before you rush out into the garden with a net and a bag of nuts, there's a reason you don't see a lot of people with pet squirrels . . . their teeth!

Squirrels have some of the most fantastically efficient teeth in the animal kingdom. They can chew through wood; in fact they can chew through most things. A squirrel's front teeth never stop growing, so it needs to grind them down by gnawing on things like trees, chairs, tables, walls, floors or even your granny's wooden leg! They are also hyperactive little critters, and need loads of space to run, climb and jump about. Plus, they have sharp claws which cling to tree bark . . . or to your face! In other words, they don't make ideal pets.

93

No. 3: BIG CATS

NOVELTY VALUE: 8 out of 10

Not many people are brave or stupid enough to own one.

MAULING VALUE: 10 out of 10

If you think a squirrel sounds a bad enough pet, what about a big cat . . . and I'm not talking about a chubby tabby with a big belly. I mean lions, tigers, leopards and cheetahs. They can definitely give you more than just a scratch!

TOTAL: 18

Actress Phyllis Gordon and her pet cheetah in 1939.

In the past, when there weren't any laws to stop you keeping man-eating pets, you could pop down your local shop and buy a lion. That's what happened in 1969, when two friends went to Harrods department store in London and bought a lion cub. They called him Christian and kept him in the basement of their own shop. But he was eventually returned to Africa and released.

His owners had realized that big cats, even the most cuddly ones, belong in the wild, not in your house or shop. Adult lions and tigers grow to the size of a sofa, eat around 15lbs of raw meat a day and, to mark their territory, spray wee on everything – including you.

Christian the Lion chilling out in the back of a car.

But though Christian seemed to enjoy his new surroundings, he never forgot his life in London. When his owners went back to Africa to visit him a year later, he not only recognized them, but jumped up and gave them a big lion-y hug! The film of this reunion made Christian an internet sensation.

Most big cats aren't as friendly as Christian though. Even if you've reared one lovingly by hand since it was a tiny baby, it's likely to turn round and bite your head off when it gets to be an adult. Between 1990 and 2011, seventy-five pet owners were killed by their exotic pet animals, twenty-one by big cats alone!

WARNING – THIS NEXT BIT IS SCARY!

Most of us like to pick up our pets, cuddle them, and scratch then behind the ears. But try doing that with this bizarre pet.

No. 2: HIPPOPOTAMUSES

NOVELTY VALUE: 9 out of 10

Only a handful of people on earth keep them as pets.

BED-SQUASHING VALUE: 10 out of 10

TOTAL: 19

Did you know? Wild hippos kill thousands of people every year in Africa, more than all the lions, elephants, leopards, buffalo and rhino combined!

In Africa the Joubert family adopted a pet hippo called Jessica, who was separated from her mother and swept into the Joubert's backyard during a flood. They raised her by hand and she became part of the family. She even slept on her own double bed! When she grew up, she had to be moved outside to the patio, but still trotted inside for her nibbles, coffee and massages!

Other owners haven't had such good experiences with their pet hippos though. In 2011, a South African man was attacked and killed by a supposedly tame pet hippo which he had kept for more than five years.

BIZARRE PETS IN THE WHITE HOUSE

Most American presidents have owned a pet or two, usually a dog, a cat or a few birds. But some presidents owned weirder animals.

In the nineteenth century President **John Quincy Adams** was given an alligator. It lived in a bathroom in the White House and terrified the guests!

The Roosevelts' pony, Algonquin.

Early twentieth-century President **Teddy Roosevelt** and his family owned guinea pigs, a rabbit, a pony, a pig, a badger, a lizard called Bill, a hyena and a small bear! His son Quentin once let out his pet snakes during a very serious political meeting, which made lots of important people jump on the table.

The Roosevelts' macaw, Eli Yale.

The Roosevelts' one-legged rooster.

I still don't smell!

The Roosevelts' egg sandwich, Graham.

No. 1: ALLIGATORS & CROCODILES

NOVELTY VALUE: 10 out of 10
You'd have to be stark staring mad to keep one!

CHICKEN-SWALLOWING VALUE:
10 out of 10
They may have 80 teeth but with mouths like theirs, why bother to chew?

TOTAL: 20

Scary!

Let's face it, these scary pets can be a big problem! It's that old story – you buy a teeny-weeny baby gator, all big eyes and cute smiles, and a few years later you've got a 20ft-long reptile with a mouth full of razor-sharp teeth living in your house.

FROM 'AHHHHH' . . .   . . . **TO 'AAAARGH!'**

Alligators and crocodiles are part of the same family called the 'Crocodilians'.

You can tell the difference because alligators live mainly in the US and China, while crocs are found all over the world.

Crocodiles have a more V-shaped head than gators and are better at living in seawater.

V-shaped heads, seawater – who cares! They all freak me out!

One man in the UK shares his home with a 5ft-long Caiman crocodile. He has spent thousands of pounds making his house croc-friendly, including installing a special pond and an extra-large cat-flap!

I normally use an electric razor.

A full-grown adult male croc can weigh as much as three cars.

An Australian woman keeps three pet crocodiles in her home, lets them sleep on her son's bed and takes them for walks. To stop them fighting, each croc has its own pond – one in the lounge, one in the bedroom and one in the bath!

Owning a crocodile or an alligator is no piece of cake. They can live for up to fifty years and grow up to 20ft long.

I can't do either of those things.

Even the tamest ones are pretty grouchy.
They don't like to be touched or petted, and owners are advised to put on a tough pair of gloves and hold a long pair of tongs when feeding them. If you forget, you may end up with a few less arms and legs.

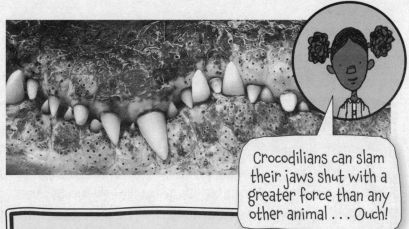

Crocodilians can slam their jaws shut with a greater force than any other animal . . . Ouch!

MONSTERS UNDER YOUR FEET

There are lots of stories about alligators living in the sewers under New York City. People say unwanted pet gators were flushed down the toilet by their owners, and now lurk beneath the streets ready to chomp anyone brave enough to venture into the sewer system.

This is actually a load of rubbish. Not only is a sewer a rotten place for a gator to live (it's too cold and dark and even an alligator draws the line at living in raw sewage), but there's no real evidence of anyone ever actually seeing one.

But unwanted pet alligators do turn up from time to time in New York – in fact they regularly appear in the local rivers. Presumably they've been dumped there by owners who don't want them any more.

Let's face it, you'd be much better off with a dog!

CHAPTER SIX

WORKING PETS

NOME MUSHERS

It was the winter of 1925, and in a remote Alaskan city called Nome, children were dying of a killer disease called diptheria. Medicine existed that could cure them, but the only supplies were 1,000 miles away, there were no roads, trains or planes, and the sea was covered in thick ice which made it impossible for any ships to reach the city.

A Nome musher and his team.

There was only one chance of saving the children's lives – use dogs! In a race against time, rescuers harnessed teams of huskies which pulled sleds over 674 miles, through icy blizzards and temperatures of minus 45°C to carry the lifesaving medicine to Nome.

The last team got lost in a snow storm, but the lead dog, Balto, found the right route, delivered the medicine safely to the city, and saved hundreds of lives!

What's a Nome musher?

'Musher' comes from the French word for 'Go!' It's what dog handlers shout at huskies to make them go faster.

Life might seem pretty easy for our dogs today. They have a nap, eat, sniff things, have another nap, scratch themselves, eat some more, and then have another nap. Then if they're feeling really adventurous, they might toddle outside for a walk or try and dig up a stinky old bone. It's not exactly hard work, is it?

Actually some of us do a whole lot more. We pull things, and lift stuff!

SLOW DOWN!

We rescue people and heal the sick!

We even dance!

We herd and hunt!

THANKS BOY!

The oldest known dog breeds were either lapdogs . . .

. . . or hunting dogs. They were trained to help bring down big animals or herd them to where humans could deliver the knock-out blow.

But once people began breeding cows and sheep for food, they didn't need to hunt wild animals as much. Even so, that didn't stop them from using dogs to chase down animals for sport; retrievers were bred to bring back dead birds that had been shot out of the sky, terriers were used to hunt rabbits, and beagles to track animals like foxes.

A 9,000-year-old cave painting of a man waiting for someone to invent the poop scoop.

WHO'S A GOOD DOGGIE?

When hunting became a rich man's hobby, dogs were bred and trained to do specific tasks. Their names give us clues as to what those jobs were.

- **'Hound'** just means 'dog'. But some dogs were bred to hunt specific animals – Wolfhound, Foxhound, Deerhound, Elkhound.

- **Pointers** and **Setters** stay still when they spot birds that are hiding, pointing with their nose so the hunter can creep up on them ('set' is an old word for 'keeping still').

- **Springers** bounce through the undergrowth to frighten birds who are trying to hide.

- **Terriers** are named after the French word for earth ('terre') and are good at digging into burrows after rats, rabbits and badgers.

- **Retrievers** collect dead birds without damaging or eating them.

Dogs aren't the only animals who've helped us to hunt.

Hurry up, my arm's getting tired!

4,000 years ago people started keeping birds of prey, like falcons and hawks, to catch small animals and other birds for food.

The ancient Egyptians used cats to hunt birds in the marshes.

Ferrets were trained to wiggle their way down holes and catch rabbits.

I don't think they've spotted me yet . . .

YUM-YUM, ROASTED RATS

In Victorian London dogs chased down the swarms of rats that infested the city. A man called Jack Black was official rat catcher to Queen Victoria. He dressed in a scarlet coat and waistcoat, and wore a huge leather belt with cast-iron rats fixed to it. He was covered from head to toe in scars from being bitten by rats and nearly died three times from infected bites. He even ate roasted rat, which he said was as *'moist as rabbits and quite as nice'*. But it was his terrier Billy who did all the hard work. He sniffed out the rats hidden under the floorboards, and down the sewers, and made his master famous!

NIPPERS AND BARKERS

Nowadays one of the most common careers for dogs is herding. Farmers often use them to round up large herds of animals like cows, sheep and goats. They run round the animals, nipping, barking or just looking scary to keep them together and make them move in a certain direction.

Sometimes they do this over very long distances. In Australia, cattle dogs help move thousands of cows over enormous distances to market or to fresher pastures. It's tough work in harsh terrain and scorching hot weather, all the time dodging the hoofs and horns of angry cows!

Dogs like these often have a natural herding instinct. If there aren't any cows or sheep around for them to herd, they'll often round up anything they come across, like cats, ducks, chickens, children and even cars.

In Australia, one owner watched as his plucky pooches herded some sharks that were basking in shallow water!

And if you think all that sounds like hard work then just consider the dogs that save lives for a living!

A Belgian milkwoman on her rounds, 1922.

Throughout history, if you couldn't afford a horse, a donkey or an ox, you tied your dog to a cart and used it for transport. Dog carts were a popular way of delivering fresh milk, bread, fish and meat, and collecting rubbish, because they could fit through alleyways too narrow for a horse. Not only that, the dog could be used to guard the load!

There was a much worse job though that dogs, were made to do. In medieval kitchens, small dogs, called 'turnspits', had to run in a wheel that turned big chunks of roast meat over a fire. This was not only exhausting, sweltering hot work, but imagine how frustrating it must have been. The dogs could smell the lovely whiff of roasting meat, but it was always just out of reach!

A lot of jobs animals had to in the past do seem to us now to have been very cruel. In Roman and medieval times, dogs were made to fight other animals – bears, bulls and badgers. People would watch and bet on which animal would win. In England, King Henry VIII had a special arena built at his palace in Whitehall for 'bear baiting'. A bear was chained to a post in the centre, and groups of dogs were sent in to try and kill it.

I wish they'd hurry up and invent the RSPCA.

Don't worry, it's on the next page!

Eventually bull and bear baiting were banned, but that wasn't the end of the cruelty. People were soon training dogs to fight each other.

HUMANITY DICK

Until recently, experts thought that animals didn't feel pain like we do. This was because animals can't talk and so don't say things like *'Ow that hurts'* when you stick them with a pin.

Sensible people have always thought this is rubbish. Anyone who knows anything about animals can see that they avoid doing things that cause them pain – for example by running away from people who hurt them.

But because so many people thought animals didn't feel pain, cruelty to them was pretty common before the nineteenth century. Not only were animals made to fight each other for entertainment, but many animals were regularly starved and whipped by their owners.

As more and more people started keeping pets, attitudes slowly changed, and eventually a law was passed to try to stop anyone from hurting animals.

One man in particular helped to change the law – Richard Martin or 'Humanity Dick' as he became known. He hated animal cruelty – he once challenged a man to a duel for killing a dog. He came up with the idea of making cruelty to animals illegal and wrote the first law against it in 1822.

Two years later he got together with a group of like-minded men and founded the 'Society for the Prevention of Cruelty to Animals'. Their aim was to persuade people to care about animals and to gather evidence about those who abused them. In their first year they helped to convict sixty-three offenders!

In 1840 they got the support of pet-loving Queen Victoria and formed the '**Royal** Society for the Prevention of Cruelty to Animals' or RSPCA – today the oldest and largest animal welfare organization in the world.

What a bunch of asses!

A DOG CALLED HAIRY MAN

In 1828 a ship full of Irish immigrants bound for Canada was wrecked in a gale off the coast of Newfoundland. A local fisherman, George Harvey, heard shouting from terrified people clinging to the storm-tossed rocks, and he and his family rowed out to rescue them. But they couldn't get near because of the fierce waves. So their dog Hairy Man jumped into the water and swam to the rocks with a rope between his teeth. 163 people were pulled off the deadly rocks and saved. Well done, Hairy Man.

Newfoundland dogs have got thick waterproof fur and webbed paws. That's why they're such powerful swimmers. They are so strong they can pull twelve people through the water at the same time!

In Italy, Newfoundland dogs have been trained to jump from helicopters into the sea to rescue people!

ANOTHER DOG CALLED BARRY

High in a remote pass between Italy and Switzerland is a monastery called the Great St Bernard Hospice. The monks there owned big dogs which rescued people trapped by storms and avalanches. These St Bernard dogs sniffed out injured travellers, dug them out of the snow and lay on them to keep them warm until help came! One St Bernard called Barry saved the lives of over forty people!

And though dogs can be good at rescuing people . . .

For instance, Buddy the German Shepherd dialled 911 and whimpered for help when his owner Joe fainted!

Other animals can do the same thing . . .

Willie the parrot flapped his wings and screamed 'Mama baby' to alert people that a two-year-old girl was choking.

Winnie the cat woke her owners to warn them that poisonous carbon monoxide gas was leaking into their home at night.

Until 1986, British coal miners used canaries to let them know when there were poisonous gases in their mine. Canaries are more sensitive to these gases than humans, and could act like an early warning system. If they became upset the miners knew they had to get out quickly!

119

PETS AT WAR

Some pets have even been involved in fighting wars.

Simon the Cat served on a Royal Navy warship during World War II. He helped to keep the sailors happy . . .

> . . . by purring, playing and generally looking cute.

He also stopped the ship being overrun with rats. He was badly injured during an enemy attack, but survived and became a celebrity back in Britain.

> Simon got all the glory, but there were loads of us on board ships.

Rip the Terrier was found wandering round London by an Air Raid warden during the Second World War. He became one of our first search and rescue dogs and sniffed out people who were trapped under fallen buildings after explosions. In just one year he rescued over a hundred casualties!

Commando was one of about 250,000 pigeons who served in World War II. Commando made more than ninety trips into occupied France with a little canister tied to his leg full of top secrets. He flew all the way there and back, dodging German guns and birds of prey which had been trained by the Germans to kill messenger pigeons.

And now . . .

A real dog hero . . . !

A great dog hero . . . !

The greatest dog hero of them all . . . !

Sergeant Stubby! He was a pit bull terrier.

He liked chewing bones . . .

. . . and weeing on lamp posts.

But when he became part of a regiment of American soldiers in World War I . . .

. . . he turned into a super-hero!

He found wounded soldiers, he warned his unit when he smelt poison gas or heard falling bombs.

He caught a German spy by biting him on the leg and making him fall over! He took part in seventeen battles and won lots of medals for bravery.

Sergeant Stubby shows off his medals.

122

HERO RATS

No rat has ever won a bravery medal, but they still put their lives at risk detecting deadly landmines. Rats have a fantastic sense of smell, can be trained easily because they're smart, and are lightweight so they don't set off the mines. Landmines lie hidden for years after wars are over, so rats like this one save lots of human lives!

A hero rat sniffing out a landmine.

LENDING A PAW . . .

Most pets don't have to jump out of helicopters, sniff landmines, or dodge bullets to be lifesavers. For some people, their pet is a lifesaver on a daily basis, helping them to cross the street, open doors, eat lunch or go to the loo. Without their pets, life would be much harder for such people.

Or hoof!

123

The blind have used dogs to guide them for centuries, but the first official 'guide dog' training school was opened in Germany during World War I when a doctor had the brainwave of using dogs to help soldiers who had been blinded in battle.

Today dogs aren't just trained to help blind people by guiding them around obstacles . . .

- They help deaf people by alerting them to important sounds like the doorbell or a smoke alarm . . .

- They help disabled people by picking things up or pulling their wheelchair.

And it's not only dogs! Some blind people use miniature horses as guide animals.

. . . because we're calm, can see well, are easily trained and live longer than a dog.

A seeing-eye horse in America.

124

Parrots, cats, ducks and at least one iguana help their disabled owners get on with everyday life.

DIABETIC ASSISTANCE DOG

Dogs have such an excellent sense of smell they can even detect minute changes in the medical conditions of their owners.

Lola's owner Liz is diabetic and does not have the usual warning symptoms of low blood sugar, so she could collapse and become unconscious. Lola has been trained to alert Liz before her blood sugar becomes dangerously low, so that she can take some glucose.

Dogs like Lola have been trained to help children with the same problem – they accompany their owners to school!

www.medicaldetectiondogs.org.uk

THERE, THERE

Anyone who has a pet knows how nice it feels when you play with them or give them a cuddle. Some dogs, cats, birds and rabbits work as 'therapy animals', going round hospitals and helping to cheer up poorly people. By getting them relaxed and having fun, the animals help the sick to recover.

PETS IN PLAYS

Some animals earn their dinner by roller-skating, tightrope walking, dancing or performing in front of a camera for films and TV.

For hundreds of years troupes of acrobatic and dancing dogs toured villages and towns around Europe entertaining the crowds.

In the 1890s doggy stars included a poodle known as the 'Inimitable Dick' who danced on his hind legs while wearing a dress, and a 'dog orchestra' of dogs playing drums, cymbals, the violin and the trombone. Dogs like 'Munito the Wonderful Dog' were trained to play cards, do maths and spell words.

Some dogs were even actors. In 1891, in Paris, you could see a dog show in which a building burst into flames and a poodle in a night dress was rescued by poodle firemen aided by a small fire engine.

Parrots were also trained to do tricks and perform for crowds. Because they're intelligent and love a bit of fun, they could be taught to roller-skate, ride tiny bicycles and drive little cars.

In America in the 1960s, a woman called Alba Ballard put clothes on her pet parrots and cockatoos and took photographs of them. She dressed them as baseball players, boxers and golfers; one was a tiny feathered pianist, another pair rode a motorcycle. Today most people don't like that sort of comedy, but in the 1970s and 1980s audiences thought it was hilarious and her parrots regularly appeared on television. She even made films, including one called *The First Bird on the Moon*, in which a parrot descended from a lunar module and landed on a replica moon!

Showbiz is my life, darling!

If you try and persuade most cats to do a trick, you're likely to get a dirty look or a swipe round the ear. But 'cat circuses' have been around for years. The performing pussies walk along tightropes, teeter on mirrored balls, jump through hoops and balance on their front paws.

SHOWBIZ DOG

The invention of cinema opened up a whole new world for performing pets. Some of them became international celebrities. One of the most famous was 'Lassie', a lovable collie dog who rescued accident-prone children from burning buildings, avalanches, rock slides and swirling rapids.

Kids went crazy for all things Lassie; there were Lassie books, games, comics and puzzles.

Lassie wasn't her real name. She was played by Pal, a highly trained male dog who could sit, dig, crawl, lie down, eat, drink, open doors, jump walls, play dead, climb, scratch, yawn and bark on command. At other times he needed a little persuading – for example when the script wanted Lassie to jump up and lick his owner, they had to cover the actor's face with ice cream!

Pal was paid around $1,000 a week – more than some of Hollywood's biggest human film stars of that time!

Pal as Lassie in *Lassie Come Home*.

CHAPTER SEVEN
DOGS IN SPACE

The first living creature ever to be fired into space was a dog!

A dog?

Why on earth did humans send a dog?

In the 1950s and 1960s no one knew whether a living creature could cope with space travel without being squashed or becoming horribly ill. So Russian scientists decided that before putting human astronauts into space, they'd send some dogs up to see whether they'd survive.

Where did they get these poor dogs from?

They were strays who'd been found on the streets of Moscow.

It can't have been much fun for them!

No. As part of their training, they had to sit in small boxes for up to twenty days at a time.

Lots of them did and had a big fuss made of them on their return. One mission in 1960 nearly ended in disaster when an engine failed and the rocket plummeted to earth, crashing in the Siberian wilderness in freezing weather. When the rescue team found the wreckage, the dogs were cold and exhausted, but despite their nightmare journey were still alive!

But dogs aren't the only pets who have been forced into horrible situations because humans wanted to find things out.

What about us?

Admit it – you can't resist my cuteness . . .

Nobody knew hamsters even existed until 1839, when they were discovered living happily in the Syrian desert. A hundred years later in the 1930s, a few were taken to a scientific laboratory to be studied.

Scientists found there were lots of similarities between the insides of a hamster and the insides of a human being. This meant they could test drugs on the little creatures and work out roughly what the effect would be on a person. Hamsters became more and more useful. They were friendly to humans, easy to keep, and quickly produced more hamsters – so they could be replaced really quickly. Within a few years they were being used in laboratory experiments all over the world.

135

Scientists don't just experiment on hamsters. They use lots of different kinds of animals.

We're the most widely used lab animal.

Scientists like to use mice because there are lots of them, they're small, easy to handle and cheap to care for.

That's stupid! Why use mice? They're nothing like humans!

They are. We share over ninety per cent of our genes with mice.

In other words the building blocks that make up a human and those that make up a mouse are ninety per cent the same! They're really useful test subjects.

Wow, I'm ninety per cent mouse!

In the nineteenth century, when people were looking for cures for killer diseases, they deliberately gave them to guinea pigs and then tried out various ways of curing them.

Ouch!

Yes, we've really learned a lot from these kinds of experiments — hip replacements, kidney and heart transplants, anaesthetics, penicillin and blood transfusion all rely on animal research.

Rubbish! It's not reliable! Animals in labs get stressed, and this can affect the results. Come on! We live in a modern age now. Use computer modelling instead.

Experts have recently developed a way of curing deafness in gerbils. They say one day this technique may help deaf people to hear again!

Rats are tested, not just to help cure diseases, but also to see how the brain works. For instance, they're sent round mazes to help work out how our minds remember routes and pathways.

Often companies create new products like lipsticks or shower gel that they want to sell in shops. But because they contain lots of chemicals, the people who make them don't know if they'll burn our skin or make our hair fall out. To find out more about their effect, scientists in the past used to test them on an animal first – usually a rabbit. Lots of people have protested about this because the tests often hurt the animals forced to take part.

Huge rabbits protesting about their treatment.

GOOD NEWS

In Britain it's now against the law to sell cosmetics that have been tested on animals! Hooray!

Let's face it, none of us would choose to be a lab animal – their life is often short and painful. You might be shot into space, or have an ear grown on to your back, or be sent round endless mazes in a glass box. And yet without such animals we wouldn't have lots of the life-saving medicines and ingenious inventions.

So is testing on animals right or wrong?

WHAT DO YOU THINK?

BIP BIP BIP

MORE GOOD NEWS!

Science doesn't always cause animals pain. It can help them too . . .

In the past when a pet lost a leg in an accident, or was born with a disability, its future was bleak. But today, injured or disabled pets are being given a second lease of life.

MEET THE BIONIC PETS!

Oscar the Cat – Oscar lost his back legs when he got them caught in some farm machinery. Surgeons implanted two metal pegs which act like new legs and help him walk.

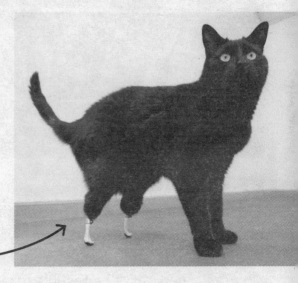

Patch the Guinea Pig – when Patch lost the use of his back legs, a friendly engineer made him his own wheel chair, using the remains of a toy car and a skateboard kneepad.

Naki'o the Dog – Naki'o developed frostbite after he was left in a frozen puddle. He lost all four feet but thanks to pioneering surgery he now has new feet to help him on his way!

Gamera the Tortoise – Gamera had his leg amputated after suffering severe burns. A swiveling wheel glued to his shell now keeps him on the move!

PET CLONES

We all know our pets will eventually die. It's very sad of course, but now scientists have invented something that could put a smile back on your face. Why not clone your pet? Yes – it's possible to make another one that's virtually identical to the one you've lost!

Cloning means making a copy of an animal. It's done using its cells to produce another animal just like it. With this technique scientists can create a living replica in just a few months!

You need to be rich to have a cloned pet though. In 2009, an American couple froze their Labrador's DNA – then, when he died, paid $155,000 to have him cloned. That's one expensive puppy!

The world's first cloned cat – produced by scientists in Texas – was named 'Copycat'!

Do I have a brilliant name or what!

But it's not only scientists who've been thinking about new ideas for animals. Inventors everywhere have been busy dreaming up ingenious gadgets and gizmos for pets of all shapes and sizes.

NITS'S TOP TEN BIZARRE PET INVENTIONS

10 **Doggles** – Goggles for dogs. They are tinted so they work as sunglasses, but they can also be used with prescription lenses to help dogs with poor eyesight.

This is ridiculous!

9 **Pet High Chair** – Most pet owners don't want their pets to eat off the table. But for those who do – here's the answer!

8 **Cat Toilet Seat** – Why not put your cat's litter tray in the toilet and train it to use the loo?

7 **Pet Translator** – If you don't know what your pet's trying to tell you, get this Japanese gadget. It translates your dog's barks into messages that appear on a handheld screen . . .

6 **Cat Typing Detector** – This detects when your cat is on your computer and locks the keyboard.

5 **Dog Perfume** – To cover up the usual smell of wet dog and fox poo . . .

4 **Goldfish Walker** – Ever felt sorry for goldfish going round and round the same old tank? Now you can take them for interesting walks around the local neighbourhood!

3 **Cat Exercise Wheel** – On the other hand, if you have a cat that doesn't want to leave the house, you can give it a run on its very own wheel . . .

2 **Hamster Cars** – What hamster doesn't dream of cruising along the floor in an open topped pink convertible?

1 **Bird Nappies** – People may tell you it's lucky to get pooped on by a bird. But they're wrong. It sucks. This handy nappy is for your pet bird – so it doesn't leave any surprises down your back when you let it out for a fly!

CHAPTER EIGHT

THE IMPORTANCE OF BEING CUTE

L ook at this baby mouse.

READER'S VOICE → Ahhh! It's so cute!

It's so what?!

So cute!

We all use the word 'cute' when we see one of these, don't we?

Ahhh! Cute!

148

Or how about this?

Ahhh! cuter!

But what does 'cute' mean?
Why do we love baby kittens and
puppies and bunnies so much?

Because they're
cute!

The answer seems to be
that baby animals remind
us of baby humans, and
baby humans need to be
protected.
In other words our instinct
is to look after them – we
can't help ourselves!

The animals we find the cutest usually have round heads and big eyes like human babies. On the other hand, if an animal has slimy skin or patchy hair it freaks us out because it reminds us of a sick human.

For instance, what do you think of this blobfish?

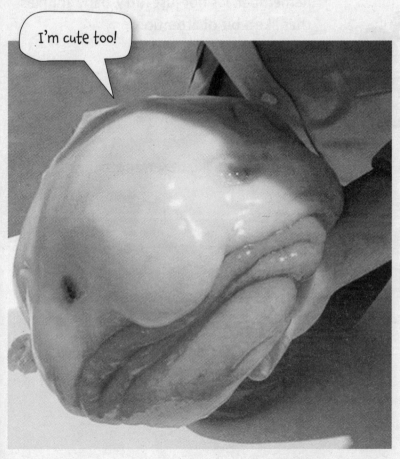

Remember, it's not just furry, baby animals that like a bit of attention.

> Yes, we know that.

So would you like to see another blobfish?

> . . . Can we see another cute thing instead?

All right, just one more time.

CUTE!!!

Pawfully good picture credits

I've surrounded myself with a grown-up version of the Curiosity Crew. They are Gaby Morgan and Fliss Stevens (Editorial), Dan Newman, Tracey Ridgewell and Rachel Vale (Design), Kat McKenna (Marketing) and Catherine Alport (Publicity). A big thanks to them all; they are committed, funny and extremely cool.

Tony has to say that otherwise they'd stop work and go home!

Are you still there? Bye-bye, everybody. Bye-bye!

Also available: